Commodore Rookery

poems by

Christy Lee Barnes

Finishing Line Press
Georgetown, Kentucky

Commodore Rookery

For Trevor,
who is so much more than a moose racing enthusiast.

ACKNOWLEDGMENTS

"I've heard": *Comstock Review;* reprinted in *Final Girl: An Anthology of
Survival* (Porkbelly Press)
"At five weeks": *Cagibi*
"Late Postpartum Dream Sequence": *Literary Mama* (Best of the Net 2023
Nominee)
"The Traveler": *The Ekphrastic Review*
"If I describe in detail…": *Poetry Is Currency*

Publisher: Leah Huete de Maines
Editor: Christen Kincaid
Cover Art: Trevor Daniel Barnes
Author Photo: Mackenzie Chrzanowski
Cover Design: Elizabeth Maines McCleavy

Order online: www.finishinglinepress.com
also available on amazon.com

Author inquiries and mail orders:
Finishing Line Press
PO Box 1626
Georgetown, Kentucky 40324
USA

Contents

Late Postpartum Dream Sequence

I am bound with thick ribbons.

Knots at my wrists,
knees, ankles, waist.
Anywhere I might break.

I might break anywhere.

Bright silk, colorful.
Constricting blood flow.

I tied them all myself.

Now pull at a loose end
until it unspools.

Now flex a naked wrist,

which is healed,
which was never broken.

At the Heron Rookery, Early Spring

I don't have it:
the neat rhythm of this mother's straightening.

One shake and all her feathers fold sleek,
a place for everything. But I do my best.

We play and play and play.
I ache with love,
I let you crawl all over me, feed me your toys.
I clap my hands and you clap back: we speak this way.
I blow raspberries, and you buzz back, happy.

We take a walk to see the nests and I say caw caw caw caw
and you say caw caw caw, clear as day,
giggling at the new sound,
whole tiny body shaking
with the pure joy of it.

This is what I know how to do. So this is what I am doing.
I am speaking between species,
I am learning to forget language,
to listen instead.
I am leaving things undone.

Dishes in the sink, boxes in the hallway, seedlings bought
but not potted, nights unslept, hair uncombed, the plastic
clamshell of pre-washed spinach gone brown. I am trying

to rest in the new softness of my body,
the cushion it made and still makes for you. I am trying.

I study her focus, throat full of food and certainty,
dipping down to feed.

And when she flies off to hunt it's the same.
Wings fanned against the pale wind, born for it.

And you cawing out to her, sure of yourself, too.
As if you knew her in another life,
so I join you.

I've heard

before the brothers got
their hands on them
the tales passed woman to woman, a whispered
survival manual:

How to wander   long enough
                              to outlast a father, brother,
devil.   How to turn fear

to feathers.   How to grow back   a limb.
How to magic a circle.   What to do   when you fail.

Not stories, but spells
to sing against the ache
of bad bargains, stolen tongues,
lost souls, swollen wombs,

plundered boats and singing bones.
Tell me those.

At five weeks

4:00 am, after pumping,
I arch over the kitchen sink

to hand express
the way the nurses taught me.

I check the milliliter markings,
watch the drops deepen their color.

Hindmilk, where the fat is.

The thin stream clings
to the sides of the cup.

I swell with pride
at its richness,
but it's still not enough.

Afterward, sleepless,

I sit by the window
with my emptiness. I watch
the first light leak in
and eat a whole bag of dried mango.

I hold each piece of fruit on my tongue a long time,

as if to pull from it something I have lost.

If I describe in detail the girl who flew away with the cranes, do you think we could find her?

Rie Muñoz, Crane Legend

I saw her at first at a garage sale
in some basement of some house we could never afford.
When I picked her up, the woman browsing beside me
named the artist. But of course I wasn't paying attention, then.
I didn't expect this to be a memory.

What I know: The ink was silvery bright
and there was a wide white border
and a blue sky and a plump girl with a sly smile and a crooked headscarf
and a flock of birds all floating up, up, up, into the clouds
and the cranes swirled around the girl almost in the shape of a heart.

Not a heart really, but the feel of it. It was cheap,
like ten dollars. Which is steep enough to give pause at a garage sale
but not enough to keep you from something you love,
but I still walked away
and now I don't know why. How do we know what we'll go on to want?

Maybe I thought if I hung it up people would talk, would say
what I want is to leave my life,
and that's not it at all,

not at all the same thing, I don't think, as wanting
to be carried off
in an almost-heart-shaped whirl of feathers
up onto a current of air and curlicue clouds until
you can look down over your life and really see it, until
everything you carry,
the life wrapped up in it all seems to weigh

nothing, nothing, nothing.

I want

the dark, lifeless wing draping
the abandoned nest

accounted for, or at least
to mean something, to be mourned. I want
to talk about it, so I try,

from a distance, through my mask. I say,

What happened? What could have happened?

A silly question, still

when the man with a fancy camera
winks and says,
mothering is hard work I guess

I laugh because
he is expecting a laugh,
then leave fast and walk home

weeping. I want
an answer
for all of this. Want
this world we brought you into
to be good to you,
to be good.

At the edge of the water, I stop
to watch listless waves
lap the canal edge and want

waves like the ones I knew
growing up: ten feet tall, loud as hell,
ready to wash everything away.

The Middle of the Story

You sleep in snow and wake up edged in gold.
You told no one your wish for fear
your words once spoken would sprout
feathers and fly off.

And you tried so hard to be good.
You tried so hard that you glowed,
but still all your magic circles
gone like chalk
after hard rain.

So you sang
of swallowing stones.
Of curses slipped loose by sly patience.

Of keys that singed your hands
with the heat   of longing.
Of cold warnings you couldn't heed.

After another storm

you weave from all those fallen branches
                a set of wings   and wait.

We Watch the Herons Nest and Talk About My Labor Again

See how her neck unspools toward a twig, watch
the thoughtless ease of her need.

     They told me it would be like that.

     Animal thing, body unhinged from mind.
     Open at last to primal purpose.

     But I with my chattering teeth,
     counting each crest of pain,
     I stayed
     agonizingly present
     as the nurses came and went,
     asking what I wanted.

By some signal we've missed
the birds all shoot to the air

like tips of flame.
Their squawks desperate, bottomless,

defense and dirge
for what can be lost.

High above the eagle circles and drifts,
scared off for now.

What It's Like

I worry   my body
      like beads   like breath   like rest
      bruised

I worry my heart slick   stomach sick
I worry the rust from the hinges worry dust

from off the tops of the bookshelves
wring worry   from the kitchen sponge
I can't ever seem
          to get clean

                breathe it in belly-deep keep
counts of eight exhale stale
        worry back out

I fill the tub with worry
       soak in it   pop a can of worry

sip from it   sudsy sticky-sweet
goes down easy

sing it tune it scale it   harmonize

suck it in
to squeeze into

last year's worry
       (two sizes too small)

I warp and weft it   pattern perfect
      pavement pound it knead it   leave it   let it rise

wrestle with it   learn its name

      limp away.

Someone here is always telling the same story

of the final attack and how after that
they fled their long-time
home in the Kiwanis Ravine
to start over here at the Locks.

I'm watching the chicks
fight for their supper,
as you sleep on my chest,
snug in your carrier,
feather-breathed and heavy.

Beside me a man
starts in: *you know they used to nest a few blocks over* ...

I do wonder
if they mark a grief like that,

if they remember.

But it doesn't matter, does it?
We are telling it for ourselves.

Night Poem

Someday you will be older.
The world will not be on fire.
At least, not this fire.
Someday we will all sleep through the night.

Tonight, you nuzzle against me,
fuzzy-headed, snuffling,
nodding off against the bottle.
Tonight, I sink into the couch
under your small, determined weight.
I'm bleary with the brilliant glare
of so little sleep
and such fierce love.
Slumped into me,
you are snoring
the tiniest snore in the world.

Birthday Poem

It's so gray today but I still
        keep finding confetti

           white berries dot the dry brush
           early rain   spatters the asphalt
           a flock of starlings
           scatter   gather back
           over the hushed water

The Traveler by Liubov Popova
At the Norton Simon Museum

They reconstruct me so cheerfully.
To them it is an act of love:
to find me as I once was,
to return me to it.

There, see? A woman on a train.
See, of course, her pearl necklace!
There she is, reading a newspaper.
She clutches her umbrella.

Look, see, she is not so broken!

But when someone comes by
and sees not a woman
but a ruined city smoldering

or a spring lake in thaw
or a curtain rising or a ransacked ship
keeping to its course or
Mt. Sinai with its holy thunder,
do not correct them. Only listen.

Aubade

In the early morning my husband
regales me with a play-by-play
of the sex dream he's just had:
We were watching moose racing
from fancy little box seats,
just giving it to each other.
I make him tell me every detail
he can remember until we
are shaking with laughter.

The milky October light
spills through the blinds,
little circles on the carpet, the comforter.

The baby is ready for his bottle, he sends
little caws and morning growls through the monitor.

A song of certainty for the day,
of the good things he is sure it will bring.

Evening Visit

Quiet now, and I've come alone.
Late light through leaves, lush and slick between
thicket shadows. Nests still, strange lull

as siblings nestle, pressed together, useless
wing to useless wing.

There behind the cement shelter
at the edge of the park

I see a shopping cart tucked in,
hear a settling cough and some sighs.

Someone is bedding down for the night.

His sounds as he eases toward sleep
have so much
of the same tenderness
of my little son
when he settles in against my chest. What trust
it takes, this life.
All of it.

Christy Lee Barnes is an educator and poet from Los Angeles, now transplanted to Seattle, Washington, where she lives with her husband and son. After earning her MFA in 2013, her publications have included *McSweeney's, Spillway, Stirring, Plume, Prairie Schooner,* and *Tin House.* She was a two-time Best of the Net nominee in 2023 at *Literary Mama* and *Mom Egg Review* and a contest finalist for *Ruminate's* Janet B. McCabe Poetry Prize as well as the *Gigantic Sequins* annual poetry contest.

She's a proud public school educator, having worked for over a decade teaching English to multilingual learners in Southern California, as well as a WITS poetry teacher in Seattle Public Schools.